Salmon Fishing on the Nipisiguit

by

Warren A. Reed and Henry K. Burrison

Watercolors by Winslow Homer

1874

as written for the

East Boston Advocate

Natural History Map of New Brunswick

1873

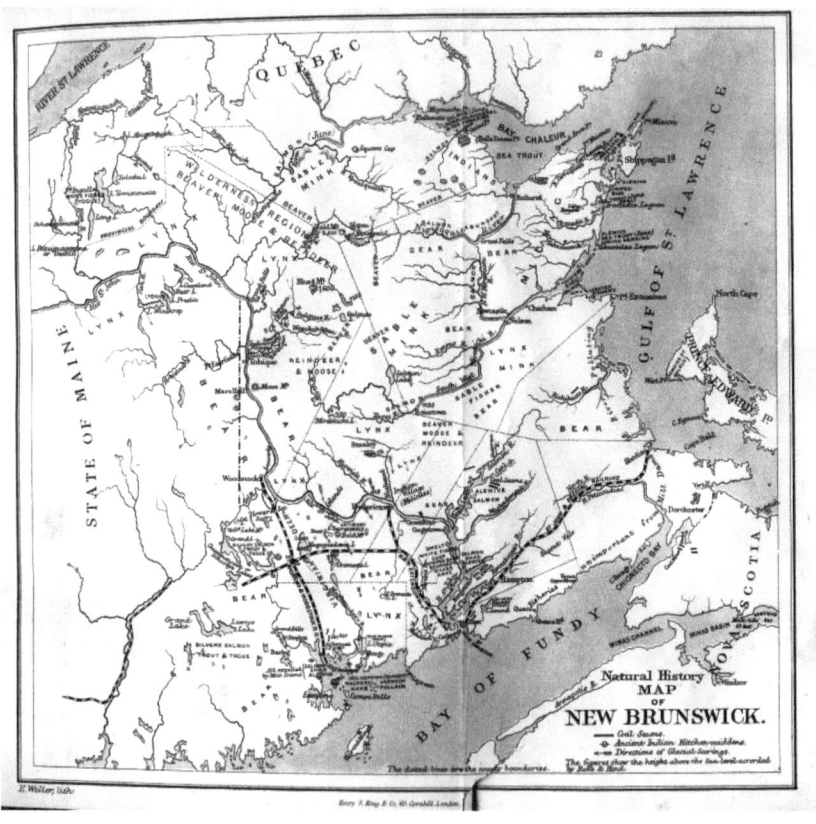

Dramatis Personae

"Old Man"	W.A. Reed	"John"	John Chamberlain
"Cook"	H.K. Burrison	"Joe"	Joseph Vienno
"Donnick"	G.H. Reed		

Introduction

This is an account of a canoe trip across the province of New Brunswick by three young men of East Boston in the summer of 1874. These articles come to us as newspaper columns in a 6 x 8 pasteboard notebook. They come with two letters loose in the front which are explanatory. Lawrence, the recipient, was the older son of Warren A. Reed. The letter is undated, but the tone suggests it was written after the death of Warren A. Reed in 1927.

65 Crescent Ave.
Jersey City Heights
July 31st

Dear Lawrence

Yours of the 25th with enclosures was duly rec'd and I at once signed the statement of withdrawal and sent it to Mr Rogerson. Speaking of the New Brunswick trip that Henry Burrison, your father & myself took in 1874, I have just read the printed a/c of it in the E. Boston Advocate, which was written by Henry & your father & taken from a little note book I kept on the trip. Did your father save the articles from the news paper? If not I would be glad to send you mine. They were never finished as both writers were busy in college & the last half of the trip (which was the most exciting) was never written.

Sincerely,

Geo Howard Reed

Lawrence Reed, the addressee, Harvard '07 and Harvard Medical School '13 was a physician in Plymouth, Massachusetts and an enthusiastic fisherman and sportsman. He had a reputation of being somewhat casual in his handling of sporting equipment, especially guns.

Warren Augustus Reed, Harvard '75, Harvard Law School '77 was the lifelong secretary of his class, a lawyer in the shoe manufacturing boomtown of Brockton, Massachusetts, a judge of the police court who (in)famously arraigned Sacco and Vanzetti, and a devoted amateur naturalist. He was a member of the Visiting Committee to the Bussey Institute, precursor to the Arnold Arboretum.

George Howard Reed was Warren Augustus Reed's cousin. Born in 1854, he was the son of George Washington Reed, a Fire and Marine insurance agent who lived in an imposing structure at 320 Shawmut Avenue, Boston. I have no picture of George.

Henry K. Burrison was from Newton, Massachusetts. He attended Boston University and became a professor of mechanical drawing at MIT. This photo is in the collection of Academy of Natural Sciences of Drexel University, where Burrison corresponded because of his passion for entomology.

In the 1922 Annual Report of the Carnegie Foundation we find:

HENRY KINGSBURY BURRISON

Henry Kingsbury Burrison was born April 15,1849. He was graduated from the Massachusetts Institute of Technology in 1875, and two years later joined its staff as instructor in drawing. During his connection with the Institute, which lasted for thirty-seven years, with advancement in grade to assistant professor, he organized and developed the department of mechanical drawing, and was its head for a number of years.

The Carnegie Foundation granted Professor Burrison a retiring allowance in July, 1914. He died February 2,1923.

Joseph Dixon Crucible Co. Pencil Department
Jersey City, N.J., U.S.A.

Dear Lawrence

Am sending the Nipisiguit and Tobique trip as it appeared in the
E. Boston Advocate and my original diary which you might like
to read and keep also. Your father and Henry Burrison wrote the
articles for the paper & when they quit and took up their school
work in Sept 1874 the articles ended, leaving us at the
headwaters where we crossed over through the 4 Nipisiguit
Lakes to the upper Tobique. The last of it, coming down the Tob
to McDougalls house when we ran out of grub was the most
exciting. The article written in the back of the book I think was
Henrys beginning to write; mine is marked Front.

Sincerely

Geo. H. Reed

I happen to have this last mentioned diary, no bigger than 3 X 5
and written in pencil, which serendipitously arrived with a note
of its own in 2001:

Richard C. Reed

Gus,

I came across this which I think is some notes on a fishing trip
with Warren A. Reed. I don't know who the others are. It's some
memorabilia do with it what you will. Excuse the writing.

Merry Xmas

RCR

Richard Crocker Reed was my uncle.

So there are two sources; the newspaper articles and George's diary. In the newspaper account, included here as Part 1, written in sort of a wry sporting idiom, we leave the boys at the portage on Bathurst Lake, about to cross over into Nictau Lake, the headwaters of the Little Tobique.

Part 2, George's little diary, gives a fairly detailed account of the second half of the trip. It took two weeks for the boys to get from the headwaters of the Nipisiguit to the headwaters of the Tobique, down the Tobique to McDougall's (who they must have contacted in planning the trip - I think they were early settlers of Riley's Brook), then to the confluence with the St. John opposite Fort Fairfield, Maine and finally down the St. John to Woodstock, where they caught a train to Boston for $10.

The boys started home on a Tuesday, ran out of food on the Saturday, found loggers the very next day and got fed. After leaving the loggers they camped one more night above McDougall's and George walked along the river and got lost. He only walked a mile or two before reaching a cabin, but he was absolutely famished.

I think it was September 21, 1874 when they fetched up in Woodstock. The trip is about 150 miles as the crow flies. It's reasonable to think that it was 200 miles on the ground. This is a pretty significant undertaking for three young men — rough camping in remote territory. Although it wasn't exploration, the trip had all the hallmarks of lengthy and impressive canoe trips in Canada. One would call this a major canoe trip even today. Evidently the canoe was birchbark.

Interestingly, something is known of John Chamberlain, one of the guides, from

THE AMERICAN ANGLER'S BOOK EMBRACING
the Natural History of Sporting Fish
AND THE ART OF TAKING THEM
1864

By Thaddeus Norris

"Anglers from the States uniformly meet with kindness amongst the Blue noses. There is an inbred urbanity amongst those of French descent, however humble their sphere in life, which is always pleasantly remembered. One of the most agreeable days I ever spent was a quiet Sabbath amongst these primitive people, the families of my canoe men. I have inserted this little vignette, fancying that it bears some resemblance to John Chamberlain. It at least expresses his fashion of wearing his hat."

Nothing else seems to be known of Joe Vienno

The painting on the cover, *Indian Falls, Nepisiguit River 1874* is by noted New Brunswick Artist Rejean Roy and shows (l-r)

George H. Reed exercising his suspenders
Warren A. Reed writing
Henry K. Burrison cooking
Joe Vienno carrying dinner
John Chamberlain and his hat

Mt. Carleton, about 600 meters, is in the background.

Most of this information, including interactive maps and downloadable KML can be found at nepisiguit.blogspot.com

Warren C. Reed, May 2014

Part 1:

[The accompanying article is from one of a party of three young men of East Boston who are spending their vacation in New Brunswick]

THE NIPISIGUIT AND TOBIQUE

I

We started one fine afternoon in August from the pretty town of Bathurst, on Bay Chaleur, in New Brunswick, with our baggage and stores, to meet our guides, John and Joe, who were to get our camp ready at the lowest salmon pool, eleven miles up the river.

A ride of three hours through the woods brought us about sunset to the camp, where a roaring fire was already prepared. Supper over, we began to get ready for the morning's sport. The rods, which had remained in their cases since we left East Boston, were now unpacked and jointed, the lines wound on the reels and leaders and flies attached, so that at break of day we might be ready to make our first cast.

We were all astir at five in the morning, and with rod on our shoulder and John at our side we were soon at the rocks on the bank of the river. At this point the river is about thirty yards wide or five or six feet deep, and down there near the bottom, heading up stream, we could see the salmon - great fellows from ten to twenty pounds weight - perfectly motionless (except the gentle waving of the tail), lying in rows in the eddies of the rocks.

The water is as clear and pure as crystal, and we could see the slightest motion. Every now and then one rose and jumped his length out of water, then sank slowly back, followed shortly by another. But we couldn't stop long to watch these beauties; we wanted to try a cast. The first was an utter failure; you can't deceive the salmon by that thing tearing through the water at the end of the leader. It looks as much like a kraken as a fly. "Another cast, more gently," suggested our piscatorial advisor, John, at our elbow. And we succeeded somewhat better. Soon we have acquired some little skill and may look for a "rise." We notice as the fly moved with hops over the water one of the salmon rose a little above the others, looked at the fly greedily and fell back among the rest. Another cast nearer to him; he started up, made a rush, grabbed the fly, and at the same instant, by a magic turn of the wrist, we struck him and had him hooked.

And now if we had a dozen pair of hands and as many eyes, we could use them all. We must look to the fish, to the tip of the rod, to the reel, to the line, to ourselves, to see where we are stepping, for soon the fish will have us running down river on rocks, through bushes, in a mad race for his life. Then he jumps full three feet clear of the water, sending a shower of shining drops around: another jump, still higher - "Lower the tip of your rod, or he will break your tackle;" and scarcely have we obeyed the ever-present John then the salmon is shooting down stream like lightning. "Let him out-let him out!" cries John and the line whirls off the reel. Down the stream he goes, and we after him, jumping, slipping, sliding over the rocks, any way to get along; and still the reel is clicking off the yards of line. He stops; no he is off again, and we following. Fifty, sixty yards have gone, and now he begins to slacken his pace. We have a moment to breathe, and John, who has been scrambling over the rocks after us with his gaff, yells at us to "reel him in." In he comes, and as yard after yard goes on to the reel we begin to see him down there taking a rest for another rush. Ha! he's off again, and the line goes "zip, zip" off the reel. Now he is into the air, throwing himself clean out of the water; and now he is tearing down the river again. "Scramble quick! hold fast to the rod! keep the strain on the tip! give him the butt of the rod or you'll lose him!" "There! he is stopping again: now reel in for life!" Well done; he is getting tired, and we can reel him in quite close to the shore.

As he comes slowly in John creeps down to the edge with the gaff; the salmon sees him and makes another rush. His fire is not gone yet and he is not so easily caught "Now reel him in again," and as he comes in we get the gaff into him, run up the bank and lay him on the green sward.

All has been excitement, but now we can stop and enjoy our prize. He is large for this season of the year - fourteen pounds. Be sure you will not soon forget that sight as he lies there, glistening in the sun on the bank of the river, which foams and dashes along, surrounded by a background of hills and forest trees. We have our first salmon and feel paid for a journey of over seven hundred miles, even if we killed only this one fish.

The excitement of salmon fishing can never be forgotten; it is not to be compared with the manual labor of pulling in a cod, or even the more boisterous sport of blue-fishing. In place of the cod-line, strong enough for an anchor road, you have the fine silk-braided line and slender rod, which seem absurdly weak to kill a salmon of twenty or thirty pounds; yet that's the art. And so the sport went on. Sixty pounds of salmon and a corresponding amount of excitement and enjoyment was the result of our morning's sport. All our troubles and trials were amply repaid. Black flies, punkies, mosquitoes, cold nights, every thing! - we would encounter these all a hundred times for such sport.

We go back to camp at peace with all the world, and wondering what people can find in the world to grumble at. B.R. [Burrison Reed, I think - WCR]

THE NIPISIGUIT AND TOBIQUE

II

[The article published a few weeks since, on "Salmon Fishing on the Nipisiguit,' was so acceptable that we are glad to announce a series of letters on the same subject from the pen of the same author. We believe they will prove interesting.-Ed.]

13

The Nipisiguit is said to be the roughest stream in New Brunswick, full of rocks, shoals and rapids, and on this account the Indians gave it the name, Nipisiguit, signifying "rough water." There are three of us the "Old Man" "Donnick" and the "Cook," two canoe men, John and Joe and two canoes. We are twenty miles up the river at Grand Falls, and here we strike and land our last salmon. Getting ready to start for the head waters, which are about eighty miles into the wilderness, we have already carried one canoe over the mile portage around the falls.

At this point the river is contracted, and with rush and roar forces its way through a narrow channel, between high rocky cliffs, in two pitches, the first boiling and foaming, the second a clear, clean fall of thirty feet. One day we go above the rush of water on the cliff, and looking down 100 feet we see it all. Far below, over a point of rock which juts out from the cliff, a foot clear of the torrent the trout are jumping. Over the point they come, clear out of the water. Look! there is one-see him jump! Hibla! there is another and another, and still another. Ah! that is a big one! Did you notice that little one from the eddy behind the rock - over the top - a clean five feet jump, striking the foaming, boiling water, to be carried down stream into the eddy and then try it again. And still others try it, some striking the rock and falling back. Better than a circus. What a power must lie in their tails to resist such a seething, rushing torrent, and spring clear into the air.

We look up and the cliffs above seem to reel and topple - the motion of the water has so affected our eyes. It is at such moments that one grows dizzy, and is liable to fall from the heights. Back of us are large holes, regular bathing tubs, worn out of the solid rock, filled with cold spring water. Here is one - the rim is circular, diameter eight feet, depth six feet. A bath! a bath! and we are soon ready. The "Old Man", is the first in and — the first out. What lively motions; never knew him to be so smart before. Is it cold? Only mild ice-water. But what care we? Have we not been wading day after day in the cold water of the Nipisiguit? Care! Not we.

Oh, no; and in we go, and - out we come with a yell, putting to shame the best leap of king salmon. We certainly care not as long as we are out of that, and take good care not to fall into that water again.

Back to camp on the hill for supper; but first come see the pool opposite our landing place. Down the little narrow, crooked path we go, passing the little brook that gives us ice-cold spring water, and are on the rocks 25 feet above the river. Over there is the pool. See! where the water is rushing in a clear smooth current, broken only by "Sandpiper" rock, and where the little ledge of solid rock is, and those two rows of dark objects! Salmon! One,-two,-thirty,-sixty in that small space. A gleam of silver, the form of a large salmon in mid air, a splash, and the river flows as before, only soon to be broken by another. Yes; John says two hundred and more have been counted in that same place, and we swallow the two hundred. Below there are others, dozens of them, but the water is deeper and we cannot see them so plain.

All night, when awake, we hear the fish jumping. A mile above us falls are roaring. Did you ever, on some still night, hear, from a distance, a train of cars rumble over a bridge? Listen! -the sound increases-the train is on the bridge, and the roar of the surging locomotive, and the train with its fearful momentum is heard, rushing with full speed over the sounding structure. The sound dies away in the distance, again to be borne by the breeze in our ear. We almost listen for the whistle. And so through the night. Crescendo and diminuendo. We think of Hiawatha: "Hear a rushing; hear a roaring; hear the falls of Minnnehaha, calling to me from a distance."

But our last salmon. The next morning we decide to try the upper pool, so squatting down in the middle, John and Joe with vigorous stroke put us up stream between the cliffs that hang high above us. Creeping close to the right bank, around rocks, into swift running water, up we go, cross to the left, and we come to a large rock that forms part of the cliff. Over the sides of the rock strips of birch bark are hanging, to prevent the canoe from rubbing, and here we land, for just above is a favorite pool. Between this rock and the right bank the water pours with fearful violence, so that it is next to impossible to force a canoe up farther; but we are safe in the lee. Out we get, climbing over the immense boulders, and from the rock making cast for the king of game fishes lying below us. But the king is tired of the sight of so much fly, and it is only after much coaxing and trying that he is hooked.

The "Old Man" has one! Zip! zip! The salmon starts up stream as if he were in a hurry, or something had come across his brain to remind him of the beauties of the stream further up. The "Old Man" is in a hurry too, and we see him follow the line that stretches fifty yards off. The line suddenly slacks. He is off! No, he turns! Reel in lively! Back he comes - passes us - and goes down the swift rushing water past the rock where the canoe is tied, into the pool below. Take care of the line or he will rub it against the rock and escape and Donnick runs forward, leans out over a high rock, takes the line in his fingers, plays the fish, while the "Old Man," with straining rod, his eye on the tip, reels and tries to turn him.

He makes one turn, and starts down stream, taking almost every inch of line. Quick! into the canoe! The "Old Man," tumbles in, John and Joe spring to their stations, the rope is cast off, and like a young steam tug the salmon draws them down stream. We see them disappear down stream, the guides paddling just enough to keep up with the salmon, the "Old Man" with rod bent like a hoop, and his eyes sticking out of his head as if he were crazy. Oh! that we too were crazy.

In fifteen minutes they all come back and we are sure of salmon for dinner for there is evidence of a fifteen-pounder with silvery scales staring with stupid eyes from the bottom of the canoe, after a chase of half a mile or more. Back we go, pleased as little children, with broad smiles over our countenances, thinking of the repast to come.

B.R.

(To be continued)

THE NIPISIGUIT AND TOBIQUE

III

After dinner John and the Old Man start out to look for partridges, while Donnick and the Cook take the canoe and try for trout. We start up stream, and for a while all goes well, but here where there is an incline the water naturally runs faster than elsewhere, and in coming from the lee of a rock we are struck by the current, and in spite of quick, hard padding, are swept down stream. We try again, putting forth more strength, but our progress is backward and soon we are looking up stream at our old starting point. Again, and with groan and puff, we paddle, doing our best. For a while the canoe is stationary with regard to the rocky banks, the water rushes swiftly past, and our labor seems in vain; then we move-inch by inch, up we go, and are floating in the slower current above. A few strokes more and we are at the well-known rock above. Tying our ark we clamber over the rocks, and make ready to entice the trout.

"Shoes off," and we are in our stocking feet, ready for the rough climb. First, in this pool from broad, flat, safe standpoint, and now the fun commences. When a slack comes we start for a point a short distance above. "Here! slide down this rock" (said rock making an angle of 85° with the horizon). After sliding about eight feet, quietly let one foot step on that projection of four square inches; let yourself go and then you are safe on a standing place about one foot square.

Above are almost vertical cliffs, 150ft high with tall naked spruces and pines clinging to the top. What if that 100 ft. pine above should carelessly let itself turn over in a reckless manner and spit one of us, after gaining a velocity consequent from falling 200 feet? We should be like a beetle that a naturalist pins down and boxes up for show. But we decline being spitted, and proceed with a more interesting part of the show.

"Cast here below, in the foam close in to the rock" The fly is skimming over the top of the water, disappears in the foam, and then is lost to our view down the throat of a trout. A jerk and Mr. Trout is soon ours. Again we cast, with a rush a trout is out of water, and turns with the fly, and then the fly turns with the trout. Again the ever increasing circles are made, the mouth of one of the finny tribe at the centre, and we have another. Almost every cast we have three or four bites at once, for the friendly fly and mild mosquito pay the respects. A trout rises, and in our zeal we strike too quick and lose him, or just as we make a more scientific throw than ever a quiet, inoffensive mosquito lights on our nose, and as a large trout goes for the fly, we strike - our nose - miss the mosquito and lose the trout. But we can stand that. It is only when the gentle "skeety" returns with his insinuating ways that we are apt to have occasion to whisper soothing words and think pleasant thoughts.

But we go on, the Cook ahead, as he has been over the rocks before. Up we crawl, hugging the wall closely, catch hold where there is the ghost of a chance to put a finger - (or any other) - nail, and soon reach a shelf four feet above water, and six inches wide. Here we find more foam, more trout, more mosquito, and more pleasant thoughts, expressed in energetic language. The Cook goes on a short distance further, stepping on a small projections, clinging to little knobs and struggling as best he may, looking like a great fly crawling along the side of a house. On a crag that juts out into the stream he stands, the water rushing below. Thirty feet on the other side is an eddy, the water dark and deep, with walls of solid rock rising above. Can the trout be in such a place - in this wilderness of water? Yea! and much of them. Every cast brings an eager mouth out of the depths, and sometimes two with rapid rush spring for the deceitful little fly.

"Come on, angel Donnick. Splendid luck!" "How did you get there? I can't fly, as my wings have not grown yet." He looks at the wall, clambers up, and sticks there, - goes down again and tries in another place. By dint of hard work-tooth, toe-nail, much trembling and hugging of cold stone, he is safely landed and contentedly fishing.

One hundred feet farther up stream the falls are roaring, casting up a shower of spray and mist. The rocks are damp. The Cook starts on an excursion to the falls. John said it was impossible to get up there, but the Cook comes from East Boston; and so he clambers up thirty feet on to a high rock. Here he goes along the top of the rock, where the sun's rays do not penetrate, and where ice is sometimes to be found the year round.   With the end of his line he just reaches the water-to that rock over which, the day before, the trout were jumping; but there is so much foam and the water is so powerful that he loses sight of his line for a while, and after discovering it some distance down the stream tries to cast back to the foot of the falls. But the current of air which the falling water creates drives the line back. Only one trout is caught, and then he tries to return, clings, and clambers back to where he can look down upon Donnick quietly fishing thirty feet below. Now, to get down there, for it is the only way. That is the question. The pole is let down the trot goes next, sliding into the water. The rock here is overhanging, in a more or less degree.   The Cook looks at it, turns round, lets himself down backward, clings and holds awhile, then goes back and looks at it again. Choosing another place he tries again, clings with fingers and feels about with toes. Two feet down and then it seems as if there was no getting either way. The toes find no resting place, the muscles begin to shake, he gets one hand a little lower, clings harder and hugs closer, and begins to slide. Is he going to follow that trout intothe seething watery rush below? No, sir. There are projections below, and sliding till he strikes them, with a few more twists and turns, is safe, and appears around a corner of the vision of the alarmed Donnick, who, having heard the splash of the fish when it fell into the water, and hearing nothing more was anxiously waiting to see the Cook float down, while he should bravely rescue him with his rod and line.

Dusk is coming on, so gathering up our trout we start for camp. Easy to come here, but not so easy to get back. We try a new route, go higher up and then down. Here is a crag jutting out with a small foothold at the base. The Cook being short, with pole in one hand and trout in other, easily passes by stooping low; but Donnick is tall, there is barely room for him, let him bend his prettiest. "Did you walk there?" "I did." "Well, I have done some tall climbing in my lIfe, but I can't go that." There is danger of being brushed off, for although there is just room enough at the base, the upper part that juts out is liable to push a body's head and shoulders a little too far out, so that the centre of gravity is without support, and Humpty Dumpty has a great fall.

"Here take my rod and fish," then brushing his hair over towards the inside he grasps the rock, stoops, clutches and crawls around, and so we come to the rock we had slid down. Here we go. One foot on that little shelf, then with one hand grab a knob way above our heads, pull up our bodies, kick, pull, push and hug and the rest is easy traveling to the canoe. "Put on your shoes over those holy stockings, and come on," and we get home to eat our allowance and listen to John while he tells of the two young men who once tried this same game of climbing, and got half-way down the cliff just at night, and from there could neither advance nor recede, and so had to cling there all night, till their guides found and rescued them the next morning.

THE NIPISIGUIT AND TOBIQUE.

IV

The old man found no partridges, so we had to keep on with the fish diet, and enjoy boiled trout as best we could, for supper.

The next morning we are to strike camp and start for the head waters. From fatigue we sleep soundly, and it is only after the sun has been some two hours on its daily round when we awake to find Donnick and Joe gone, and hear the welcome sound of a crackling fire. It may have been the fatigue, and it may not have been, that caused the cook's sleep to be disturbed; but when he had stretched himself, and had limbered his jaw by a good long gape, his dim memory seemed revived, and he averred that he heard his stockings talking during the night, saying "I'll be darned!" The rest groan at him, and tumble out to the warm fire and breakfast. By the way, this reminds us of an event that happened in St. John, while we were stopping at the Grand Central Hotel, where all the "big bugs" put up, or rather put down. Donnick, in the course of events one night, fell asleep, and dreamed a dream. He was on the seashore and saw an immensely great lobster, green, with goggle eyes. A sort of an "odd fellow," as he had his claw extended waiting to give one the "grip." Donnick approached and asked the lobster a question, expecting an answer as a matter of course, and he received an answer, and then they had quite a conversation, which was related and groaned at the next morning. How we shouted and yelled, and ever after at any out of the way remark, we would say the "talking lobster is around again." To our mind it was no lobster that invaded the quiet of his babe-like slumbers, but an immense black spider that came down from his parlor on the ceiling, and roosting on beside his ear, regaled his quiet repose with tales of the sea and bloody deeds. It may have been that self-same spider that caused so many red spots all over our poor mortal frames-and it may not have been. However, that is a problem we never solved.

By the way we should have begun as novels do, by introducing the dramatis persona. For instance, Joe, who this morning tells of the wonderful smartness of our canoe, saying that it had come up the steep bank and walked half a mile into the woods, is a character, a man you would like to know. He was a small thin man, talking English or French Lingo indifferently; but in regard to his costume we are at fault in the beginning, for not a single article do we remember, except the two patches of brand new canvas which he borrowed from our humble store to enrich his pants. We would know those patches anywhere, for they have so many times caused an audible grin at the A 1, in great black letters showed forth from a conspicuous position as Joe clambered over the rocks. Joe was well marked; he was indeed A 1, one of the world's best: and still he would make mistakes now and then, like the rest of us. He was not very good at figures, for instance. We remember asking him one day if he was married. "Yes," he said and seemed to be sure of It; but when we inquired further into his family relations, and asked him how many children he had, he was a little staggered. After communing with himself a moment he replied, "Three - eh - eh - no, four. It might have been five." We got curious one day and put another poser. "Joe, how do you spell your last name?" (It was a very strange one.) He meditated a moment, and then began to grin. It was the smile of victory. Repeating the name over and over, he said, "You go into the tent, and on the bag that contains my clothes you will find it printed." We went in and found the initials J. V. Joe meant well, but he was not always exact. It was doubtless owing to his early intellectual training. We attacked him in another of our idle moments with "Joe, do they ever find any fossils along the banks of this river!" Now this was a reckless question, as the sequel proved, but we asked it in an unguarded moment. "What, sir?" said Joe; and we repeated with explanations, "Do they ever find any fossils - fossils, you know, such as bones of animals whose remains have been covered by deposits of earth, and these deposits afterwards been washed out by running water?" "Oh yes," his countenance lighting up,, "plenty of bears get washed over the falls every year, and their bones are found along the banks," replied our faithful assistant evidently wondering what we wanted with bear's bones.

For some reason or other he never called us by our names, but it was always "You feller! " "You feller!" He relied on his companion for everything, never giving an opinion without referring to John, who considered himself and was, in fact superior to the rest of the guides and canoe men on the river. John Chamberlain was born in Maine, on one of the lakes that bears the name of his father. He called himself French but he seemed to us to be that branch of the French that comes from Cork, Limerick, etc. He was of medium height, thick set and solid, faithful and honest, reputed to be the best canoe man and fisherman on the Nipisiguit. Above his broad open countenance he had the rim of his hat turned up and pinned to the top, a fashion which we afterwards all adopted. John and Joe always talked French with each other, their tongues running like young steam engines, puzzling us exceedingly. Of the rest of the party we say nothing, as photographs will be furnished for a consideration.

But to proceed with the baggage. After breakfast the tent was struck, everything packed, and then with sweaty brows, aching backs and arms, we went twice over that mile "carry," the guides taking the canoe and heavier articles, we following with all, and more too, than we wished to carry. Donnick was the only one to meet with a mishap, he falling and breaking the handle off from the "molasses" jug. John and Joe then packed all the baggage into their canoe, and started ahead, we following, bidding farewell to the falls, salmon, and easy times, for the real, rough rugged life of canoe men.

For a mile below the falls the river is narrow and deep, confined between high banks of solid rock. Just above where we are now it is wider, with depth of water scarcely sufficient to float the canoes. But perhaps some do not understand the method of going up a river in canoes. It is simply by dint of hard muscular work. A small canoe can be managed by one person, but it is better to have two-one at the bow and the other at the stern.

Each man has a pole of about ten feet in length, made from the black spruce, and a paddle. To pole you must stand up, both poling on one side. This is the way we went: Old Man in the bow, the Cook in the stem, while Donnick, with his pants rolled above the knees, in order to get out at any moment, takes the seat of honor in the middle.

After a day or two of poling we found that it was best to put on shoes without stockings, and keep the pants furled, for at the shallow places we all had to jump out and wade, pulling the canoe till water enough to float it was found. The water is clear and cold, rippling over the smaller stones, and rushing with power over and between the larger ones, "white water" being found all along. We dined at 12 on the bank where it was damp and wet, though rocks abounded. Boiled salmon, hard tack and coffee! Oh, how good it tasted! As we sit on a small stone eating, our wet, cold feet close to the fire, the smoke circling about, driving away the ugly black fly, we see about us, under our very hands, a dozen kinds of mosses, from the coarse to the extremely delicate variety; while before us is the river, gurgling over the rocky bottom; above us, and about us, over the river, tree tops are waving; the ash, the glossy birch, the spruce and cedar, all bending beneath the gentle, swaying breeze. Below are the "Narrows," through which John and Joe took our canoe, as the water is too rough for us, and only those acquainted with the channel can pass in safety, while we walked around.

But we cannot stop, and on we go, John and Joe soon getting away ahead out of sight. Oh! the hard work, the aching arm, shall we never see their canoe on the shore ahead, and the blue smoke of the welcome camp-fire? It is a little before sunset that we see them way up the river, and in some fifteen minutes are with them, to find we had come nine miles that day. Under a large spreading elm we pitch our "lean - to," and tramping down the thick, high grass, eat our supper, spread our blankets, and with a roaring fire before us, a root or two under us, try to find

25

rest in sleep. B.R.

(To be Continued)

THE NIPISIGUIT AND TOBIQUE.

NO. V

Over the tree-tops, across the river, the genial sun is sending his refreshing rays; everything is wet with the dew, the leaves and grass sparkling with diamond adornments: the cool air is rich with odors of tree and leaf, imparting vigor to our rested frames; the warm fire and aroma of boiling coffee; the soothing purling of the river; a flock of ducks flitting down stream on whistling pinion; nature in all her aspects, gay, smiling; -ah, what luxury! Such is our morning's experience - such the poetry of life in the forest. Now for hard work; now for the strain of the long unused muscle.

For almost the whole length of Nipisiguit the depth of water is only some few inches, so Donnick, with pants above the knee, is frequently wading, and sometimes all hands are in the water pulling the canoe along. The deep places only occur at intervals, and here only are the large trout to be found.

Twelve miles only, from sunrise to sunset, and we reach the camping ground John has decided on. How vividly that night comes back to us! From one of the deep holes John has captured two trout of six pounds weight, and these boiled serve for supper. Firewood abounds here - there are fallen trees, spruce and birch in abundance, and at night for a little trouble we have all the warmth needed, and at times a little more. We are lying under the lean-to, in the dirt; the top pole abounds with the usual amount of wet clothes; our assistants have placed supper to our hands; the wet shoes and stockings are before us, four feet from the fire; John and Joe, at a safe distance, smile all over, but we stick to duty - determined, as Donnick expresses it, to "manage them fish."

Supper is soon over, the dishes washed, when John, after quietly smoking awhile, steps to the fire, lights a twig, an applies it to the tindery leaves of the spruce beneath which the fire is crackling, and sending showers of sparks through the branches; and as the powder only needs the spark, so this tree, needing but the start, is in an instant, with the rush and roar of the tornado, one mass of flame, a pillar of fire, thirty feet high, while we below shield our faces and look anxious, as it is new experience to us. But the woodsman knows what he is dong, and soon the green sappy branches stop further progress of the fire. We roll ourselves in our blankets and the dirt (the Old Man visiting dreamland immediately), and are just dozing, when we become conscious of warmth - the guides, sly dogs, having piled on an additional amount of fuel, great logs ten feet long and a foot in diameter. We peep from behind the corner of our blankets and see only an immense roaring fire, extending the whole length of the lean-to. A roast, a roast, a barbeque! and we commence to sizzle. We draw up our feet, throw off our coverings, and sweat! Oh! how it poured out of us - it was a regular rum-sweat, without (?) the rum. We turn, we squirm, sweat and blister, make certain that we are not yet a-fire and with saturated clothing at last fizzle off into a sleep; troubled by dreams of pains in flesh and bone, of heat and hot places, knowing that chuckling John and Joe know well how to play a practical joke.

The next day we have another demonstration of their joking propensities. They have left us with no information in regard to the river, and are far ahead, while we approach one of the worst places in the length of the Nipisiguit called Allan's Rocks, and it is here we meet the only accident of our whole trip.

After dinner, at which we learned that the lumberman in charge of the "Bear House' had gone down the river with his dogs, as we are quietly poling, a human form surprises us, and a brawny lumberman, with a tin cup attached to a chain hung around his neck, axe in hand, asks us to ferry him across the stream he is just preparing to ford. We put him over, and the bushes close about him as he plunges into the wood.

All day long the water has been shallow and foot by foot we have shoved ourselves up against the stream, and now as the water deepens, Donnick is called on board from his walk along the shore, and takes his seat in the center of the canoe on the bottom, facing the stern, while we proceed with more caution keeping a look-out far ahead. Several places have been passed where it took all our strength to force a passage, but this is becoming worse. Far before us, we see the water coming down upon us like an avalanche.

Over the rough, ragged rocks the flood comes surging and tumbling, between boulders it rushes and pitches, shaggy heads appear in all directions, the stones and rocks are strewn everywhere. At some places the current glistens and glides in a smooth run, elsewhere, spray is dashing, and the frothing foam, like scud before the gale, comes down in a whirl and glides past with the speed of a race-horse, concealing sunken terrors and green, shining, moss covered dangers; the driving rapids roar with its hoarse warning voice and all is confusion dire. The Old Man fixes his glasses more firmly on his nose, and all prepare for a struggle that will tax the strength to the uttermost. Can we get up? Others have, and why not we? Here is the beginning of the worst. The canoe has been winding and turning between rocks, sometimes at right angles to the stream, taking advantage of every opening, and held by sheer strength in place, where progress could be made only at the rate of a few inches a minute. Now here are two rocks, just ahead, a little to the left. Just above, the clear water pours with the power of a mill sluice, and swelling up is broken into foam. Here we advance - in the lee of one we pause, then the swinging of the stern by the cook brings the bow into the current and the old man's pole goes over on the down stream side in an instant, and while he holds, another movement brings the stern around till the nose of the canoe is pointing directly up stream, and gathering our energy, with a shove we pass between, up into the smooth run, while Donnick's usual exclamation, "Great Scott!" bursts from his lips as the water surges past almost over the gunwale. Where shall we go now? We keep to the left, which is an error, but, as usual in accidents, "nobody to blame." Ahead there is only one chance, and there the water falls one foot in three. "Shall we try it?" shouts the Old Man. "It is the only place to be seen here, and we must," says the cook, while Donnick pulls his legs from under the middle thwart, grabs the side of the birch, and remarks "you can never do it" "Are you ready?" Now — with caution. Keep cool - place your pole surely - take time - push steadily till the light craft is into the water, into the almost restless fall. Now, the time for action, for quick, lively sharp work. First one side and then the other poles go, for the birch must be held square up stream, giving the current no chance in such a place to strike the side in the least.

But it is too much and we are swept down stream, almost swamping the canoe. Recovering we try again, and this is *three* much, so again we are pushed back. Here is hurry and bustle,

29

and at last the retreat is arrested and we stop to rest and view the situation with new interest. "Where now?" "Over to the right," and at great risk we start diagonally across the stream. The old man's pole snaps. Quick! and he has the reserve pole, which is immediately handed by Donnick, and then, as it is put into the water, goes down into a deep hole, leaving only the end, on which the Old Man leans, with doubled up body, far out of the canoe. The cook's pole is held, as in a vise, between two rocks, (termed a "lobster" here) and, as he tries to wrench it out, it is pulled from his hands, almost starting the finger nails, the canoe, borne by the resistless current, goes broadside down, passes over the old man's pole, tearing it from his grasp, and now we are helpless. In a second, with a rush, the canoe strikes a rock, turns over, and we all sit gracefully down into the cold water. Ugh! - as it comes up to the eyes - Oh-h-h! British waters, by a turn of luck, have the victory over Yankee pluck. The next minute the three are standing, holding the birch, looking at each other, and a ringing laugh bursts forth over the rush of the rapids. Loss, one pole and one slipper, property of the Old Man.

In a short time that canoe was up into smoother water, walked up by hand; the water bailed out by two hats; the cook's pole, which was majestically standing upright in the middle of the river, rescued by the old man, who waded out at the imminent risk of being carried off his feet, and the old routine is observed.

A.B.

THE NIPISIGUIT AND TOBIQUE.

NO. VI

"Look at the ducks!" broke from the lips of one of our number, as with clothes dripping from our capsize in the rapids, we stood in the canoe, prepared to commence poling anew. For several days we had been driving an ever-increasing flock before us up stream. These ducks breed along the river, and now the young are almost as large as the parent, but still their wings are not yet able to bear them up. At the beginning of the rough water we had frightened one, and a person who has never seen a like exhibition can form no conception of the rapidity of motion of a young inexperienced, frightened duck. Up stream, through foam and rapid, up little falls-look at him go-feet just skimming the surface, wings flapping-flap-flap-flap-chu-chu, like the churning of a paddle-wheel of a Long Island Sound steamer, with the speed of a race-horse he goes, sometimes in water and sometimes out. The flock before us suddenly move lively, and with the water flying in all directions, disappear around a bend. We soon turn it, and then, at a glance, know that our camping place is just ahead. Yes, there are the shaggy rocks, and the water breaking over and between them. "Indian Falls." Pitch after pitch, stretches far up the river, the last falling into a broad, deep, placid pool. The ducks are ahead in a mass, but they will be stopped by the falls. John and Joe, where? Ah, a blaze of fire streams from behind the rocks and descends into that flock like a thunderbolt, sending the ducks like frIghtened sheep, huddled together in a corner, formed by the fall and a large rock: again the flash like lightning, and again John with double barrel has spoken. The ducks scatter, some half flying and half swimming, disappear up stream, and the old ones take to wing.

"Here come a wounded one!" "Head him off!" Over the other side the canoe goes, but the duck turns and makes for the side we have just left.   Donnick, with a stick in one hand, leaps from the birch, pushes through the water up to his waist, and just as he is in arms-length of the bird, falls flat on his face, while the duck, with feet going at the rate of fifty beats per second (no exaggeration), leaves us to stay our laughter and shouts, and wake to the idea that the canoe is going down with the current, and on the point of striking the bank. No one thought of poling; but we recover, and take Donnick aboard, wondering why or how we did not have a second capsize when that jump from our frail bark was made.

We gather the slain, and land on a broad rock. Nun! mum! here are six sheldrakes and one black duck. A change of clothes a warm fire, and above all that, delicious hot duck stew, make us feel like new beings.

While eating supper, Joe is sitting just outside the lean-to, when, with a skip and jump, a rabbit squats beside him, within arms-length. "We will have you for a stew," says John; and crawls for his gun. But Sir Long Ears, finding the feast not to his taste, disappears with a skip into the shade.

The moon rises full, the musquash paddles across the pool, the fire crackles and glows, and so in the calm of that summer night, with the sweetness that a hard day's work gives repose, we fall asleep, with the drowsy murmuring of falling water in our ears.

Three ducks, stewed, constitute our breakfast. For a wonder, not a trout is to be found in the pool opposite our tent; why, no one, not even John can tell. Our guides had calculated well on the amount of provisions necessary to take us to the Bear House; there being now only a little coffee, salt, mustard and pork left. We make the portage around the falls, seeing a huge bear-trap and finding some snow shoes hanging on a tree, waiting for winter. By noon we are at the last vestige of civilization, Donnick, footing it through the woods by a road and the rest going by water. This heavy log structure, built to keep bears "out" and not "in," stands back from the river at the foot of a bare rocky mountain, and is maintained by a lumbering firm in Bathurst, who stock it once a year with hay, flour, pork, molasses, peas, salt, fish, etc. for the winter campaign of their lumbermen. It is in charge of two bushy-headed French Canadians, whose shanty is close by. Our friend the lumberman whom we put over the river, and who has charge of a lumbering camp at Forty-mile Brook, is with them. Three dogs greet us in a very familiar way and growl about our legs in a way that makes us smile on the curs, and pick up a club to serve as a cane. The men are glad to see us, only one man having passed this year. He was a minister, and last year came up the Tobique and down the Nipisiguit with only one poor Indian to do all the work. This last spring he reversed his trip, so we are the second party that have gone up the river this year. For over seventy miles we shall meet no one, so here we must get provisions to last us the whole trip, and we produce a letter from the owners to the men in charge, and hand it to one of the men. He looks at it, and passes; the second can't make it; the third turns it down, and back it comes-not one of them can read. We open it and read it. It is simply an order, giving the keeper power to sell us what we need of pork at 25 cts. per lb., flour at 6 cts. per lb., and molasses at 80cts. per gal. We are glad we don't eat hay, as they might charge us one dollar per pound for that. There are no scales or measures. We got our flour bag, and the men put in a quantity. "Here, John, you are pretty good at guessing just lift this." John takes the bag, lifts, takes a pull at his pipe; looks sober, gives the bag another shake, and thinks it "needs a little more" to make up fifty pounds. Just so! Pork is bought in the same way, and the molasses measured by an oil tip pail, its contents being guessed at. No complaint ever heard on our part.

We see a tub with about twenty-five trout in it, averaging two pounds, caught from the deep holes, with hooks and lines, big enough for cod, fastened to an alder stick.

Our guns are examined, and some target practice takes place, but the natives do not hit; not even John, he the great Iago - he the boaster - who could pick the head off from a partridge at fifty yards every time. He loads carefully, after much coaxing, and fires. The target receives not a scratch, although it is a board ten feet by one, stuck on end, distant about fifty yards. "too much powder," says John; and be gets his own gun. Now look out; stand aside; ah, missed again. "The ball was rammed too tight," he says; and the next time he just grazes the side. Our host puts in a handful of buck-shot, and so manages to hit. We modestly say nothing of our skill, as it does not become the victors to boast.

We are then invited to dine, and step into the shanty to a meal of "flippers," molasses, and the inevitable tea, made strong and hot enough to tear your throat out. Such luxury! no Thanksgiving ever like it! Flipper after flipper, soaked in molasses, disappears, leaving but a very small supply for the three woodsmen, who, we supposed, had been to dinner.

"John, we find we shall have to go on alone," we say. "Very well: it makes little difference to us; if you want us, we will go clear through to the lakes; if not, it is all the same. You are over the hardest part of the river."

Before leaving Bathurst, John had declared he would not attempt to ascend the river above Grand Falls, unless we took two more canoe-men; but we carried the day, although they said that it would be impossible for such green hands as we were at poling, to get up the rapids. Day by day their talk of its being too much for us grew less and less, and at last subsided; very often they admitted that we had pushed them pretty closely.

"What do you think of our getting up the river?"

"Well," says John, "you beat us; we give it up"

"Oui," says Joe, "you fellers do well, no mistake; all hard part over."

They sketch out map of the river and its branches, show us how to make bear, beaver and musquash traps; and then, after supplying them with provisions fishing tackle, powder, shot, tin-ware, etc., we shake hands, and bid the two honest fellows good-bye. They have served us well and carry with them our best wishes and the first article for the Advocate. They disappear around a bend in the river, making quick time for home, their tongues still rattling that infernal French lingo.

B.R.

THE NIPISIGUIT AND TOBIQUE.

NO. VII.

As quickly and snugly as we can, we pack our duds in the middle of the canoe and bidding farewell to our friends at the "Bear House," start up stream, and having gone half a mile decide to camp.

While searching for a camping place, we realize more strongly that we are alone in the wilderness, as we discovered in the sand the footprint of a monstrous bear, and take a long shot across the river at a mink, who squeals and disappears. Then, too we miss the services of John and Joe; for although it is on the last of August, the nights are cold, and we being green, select wood that fizzles and smokes and dies out, so that morn sees us before the sun is up, after something that will burn, and give our shivering bodies some warmth.

We eat breakfast of flippers, and pack again. Here is the nine and a half foot wall tent, in its bag; then two rolls of blankets, two carpet bags, one knapsack ,one small bag; bag of flour, pork, rosin, candles, salt, mustard, not all mixed, but pretty much so, (all but the flour being in one bag); two guns, a jug of molasses, frying pan two feet in diameter, broiler, three tin pails made to fit one inside the other, and contain four tin plates, three cups and knives and forks. Every one has an overcoat. Our light axe, from the store of our friend Taylor, on Meridian street, East Boston, occupied a prominent position, ready for use the minute we land. All those articles, added to the weight of the "middle man," sinks our canoe, and the poling becomes hard; oh so hard.

The river is more free of large stones from here to the lakes, and consequently, there are fewer rapids, but the water comes down upon us swift and strong, yet silently, and we push, in some places only to lose ground, and then again to fight our way inch by inch. We frequently get out, and walking close to the shore, pull the canoe after us.

Shortly after noon we strike "Devil's Elbow," as a very sharp bend in the river is called. The difference between going up and coming down may be noticed by this one fact. It took about three quarters of a day's work, two poling steady, to get to Devil's Elbow from the Bear House; and a day or two after one of us, having plenty of leisure, took the canoe and went back in a little over one hour.

We camp on the point formed by the crook, beneath gigantic spruces and pines, and while the Old Man is trying to put up our cloth house, and Donnick endeavoring to make a fire, the Cook goes across the silent pool, and lands on a sandy beach, with rod in hand, to try for a trout for dinner. Selecting a fly made of a peacock's feather, he casts out, each time adding to the length of the line, and at the third cast, scarcely does the feathery fraud touch the water ere it is engulphed in the hungry maw of a fish, who makes the water foam and sends the blood tingling through the veins of the excited Cook. Back starts the trout for his lair, and then as he turns a heavy strike sinks the hook, and off he starts, making rod bend and reel hum. "Old Man," says Donnick, "look! look!" and they shout, stopping their work to look at the exciting play. They yell derisively, "Hurrah, old fellow," "Give him the butt," "Give him the tip," "Easy, easy," "Let him run," "Turn him," "Give him more line," "Reel in," and other nonsense too numerous to mention. But the Cook fights it out on his line, and gradually bringing his prey into shallow water, beaches him, and running forward throws with whoop a trout of two pounds and a half high on to the sand. Another try, the water boiling again, and three pounds and a half of solid meat is landed-a magnificent trout. In a short time he is back to the tent, with seven, averaging two pounds and a half in weight.

Dinner is soon ready, and would you city folks believe it, the two trout have been nicely broiled and scarcely touched; we, with our depraved appetites, preferring flippers (made by stirring flour into water, adding a little saleratus, and then frying in pork fat), served with "lannigan," the Micmac for molasses.

After the repast, all three, with their rods, cross the stream, and there, as we pass, we see the bottom covered with large trout. We had seen far down the river the water black with "suckers," but these are game fish. Soon all three are on that gravelly beach and then such fun! Trout after trout brought to land, till at last the Old Man's pole weakened by the strain of salmon fishing, gives way as he strikes a large beauty; and we desist, as we have more than enough to eat; sixteen, averaging two and a half pounds, being added to our store. We can do this every day if we wish, but do not slaughter many, as we cannot possibly eat them.

After several days here, we set off again, and in four days reach the lake. Every day the water goes shoaler. We pass Big South Branch, Little South, Silver Brook and Portage Brook, and the river becomes nothing but a good-sized brook; we are in the cold water from morn to eve, wading and pulling our birch. Ah! just beyond that must lie the long looked for lakes; but no, we pass that to find another, and so on till we give it up. Moose tracks are plenty and bear signs abundant. One morning having slept in an old logging camp, as the Old Man is loading the canoe, he looks downstream and he sees two moose with broad spreading horns step into the river and cross not four hundred feet below him, before he had time to take his gun from the bow. He comes back to camp with Donnick, both with their guns in hand and frightens the Cook, who does not know what to make of their excited appearance. There is the same crazy look, the eyes sticking out of their heads, just as when they were astonished by the vigorous resistance of lord salmon.

"wh-wh-what is it?"

"Moose!"

And we plunge into the forest to head them off, but we do not find them, or hear a sound, they having departed as silent as ghosts.

No matter where we are when we stop, the Cook is the next minute trying for trout, and no matter where he tries he is certain to have them after the fly. The others have laid aside their poles, and do not use them again, as they have had enough trout fishing. The Old Man promises to buy the Cook a "gold pole" when he gets home, but he does not keep his word.

For some days the air was full of smoke; the "sun's eye had a sickly glare," and we expected to soon have the pleasure of seeing a forest fire; but no, a thunder shower drives us to land one afternoon, and in haste we pitch our tent, just saving everything from a drenching. A dry stump knocked down is cut to bits Inside the tent, a fire built in a hole just within one flap, and supper is served. Pieces of wood serve to fill up the hollows, and we lie down over them, Donnick curling round the fire and burning a hole in his pants. The next morn everything is bright and clear. An eagle goes screaming past, and we continue the tramp. This is the only shower we had on our whole voyage till we struck the St. John

At McFarland or Portage Brook we found an old camp, ground our axe and knives on an old grindstone, at the risk of being devoured by black flies, picked up a rope and an old pair of moccasins, and went on rejoicing. Here is where trappers, hunters or lumbermen come through from Restigouche, fifty miles away to the north.

We are now fully in the forest; for miles below, the whole country years ago was burnt over by an immense forest fire, leaving trunks and stumps standing naked and bare in every direction. Hundreds of acres are covered with large, luscious blueberries, and tracts of land seem carpeted with crimson, the partridge berries are so thickly spread.

Now here the trees are growing green and fair. "This is the forest primeval." Spruces stand as straight as arrows, and as thick set as needles in a well stocked cushion. Some cedar is four feet and some pine; birch flourishes, and once in a while is found an elm, but no hemlock. There is ahead wood enough where it has been burnt over, to last the poor of any of our large cities for the next century.

Especially about the lakes, the mountains are clothed with green, which stretches far away to the Mirmamichi, even to the mouth of that river ninety miles away, to Newcastle and Chatham, where the logs that the lumbermen get out in the winter will be sawed into boards. If the season is favorble gangs of men will be all through here, cutting and hauling and in the spring running the logs to the towns, some one hundred miles to Bathurst, where there is a large mill; some down to the Mirimachi; same down the Restigouche, or on the other side down the Tobique to the St. John, thence to Woodstock, Fredericton and St. John city. East Boston had some of the timber that once flourished here.

Last winter was unfavorable, there not being much snow; but this was a blessing to the moose and caribou, as a deep snow prevents their escape from the hunter, who with the snow-shoe, easily slaughters immense numbers. This year, on this account, they are plenty, and their tracks everywhere abound. Every little while we pass a beaver trap, showing that all this land has been trapped over in winters past.

B.R.

THE NIPISIGUIT AND TOBIQUE.

NO. VIII.

The White Mountains tourist is happy if he catches a few small trout, and almost faint with delight if a half-pound beauty is lured from his native element. Here, anywhere, the trout are plenty, and in the pools are large and bold. One day, we remember, we came to a deep place, and the bottom seemed covered with fish, although the greater portion were suckers; so the Old Man and Donnick held the canoe against the current, and the Cook commenced to haul in the trout. There was no difficulty but this -the small fry were too quick for the larger ones, and would snap up the fly when we did not want them. The ends of our poles, from the rough contact with the stones, had become worn and were somewhat "fuzzy," and as the Old Man was holding his in the water, a trout of fair dimensions and an inquiring turn of mind, came with hungry look to examine it, and tried to bite some off; and he received a punch in the nose that astonished him, yet he bit the end again and was staggered by another blow; but he kept at it as if determined to swallow the pole, and only stopped when he found his nose becoming too soft, and left us, probably thinking that he had a narrow escape of softening of the brain.

Just before reaching the lake the country is found to be fiat, with few chances for good camping places. Alders are thick, and among them we find partridges, sometimes too stupid to fly, and with a long stick could be knocked over; but our guns are out, and a meal is provided at short notice. We find it better to keep in the water all the time, as it is cool, and prevents our getting excited; then again, a place deep enough to pole in lasts only a few rods, and so we should have to get in and out at waste of time. We drag the canoe, and in very shallow places have to lift her, baggage and all, over into deeper water. This we call "grunting."

Anxious to reach the lakes, we keep on till dark, and then a fire is built and the tent pitched. One night we had partridge stew for supper, an to enrich it, having no butter, small pieces of pork, some of it lean and tough, were put in. We helped ourselves and commenced eating. The Old Man, after chewing on a lump of meat for some minutes, exclaimed "tough little fellow, ain't he?" - referring of course to the partridge; but then he was not used to such delicacies as pork and partridge,and not having a a very discriminating taste, we could not blame him. For our part the partridge was tenderer than any "spring chicken." All night long, on all sides, the "hoo-hoo" of the hoot owl is heard. The lake brought rejoicing to our hearts, as then for the first time we remain in the canoe and exchange the pole for the paddle. The first was filled to within three inches of the surface with a sort of vegetable mould or ooze, resembling wet, decayed sawdust, and made hard paddling. Part of the the lake is becoming a swamp or bog, and here the water-lily and other aqueous plants abound, giving the ducks that almost covered the surface excellent feeding. We try to stalk the ducks; but the vigilant black duck is there, and he can guess more and see through more than any of his kindred, and so with a warning "quack! quack!," flock after flock takes to wing before we are within half a mile of them. Although the form of man is seldom seen here, the ducks are far more shy than those in more civilized portions, or even in Boston harbor.

Crossing the first lake, trylng our skill on the flying ducks, as we paddle along, we enter the second, and as we land to camp, find that the axe has been left three miles back, and so two of us go for it, and one remains to fix up. On a gigantic pine, close to our camp, on the topmost branches, is the immense nest of a blue heron, the shuh-shuh gah, and often we see the crane-like form of the solitary bird, with heavy flapping wings, neck arched close to the body and legs hanging far behind. We pass over the second and third lakes, finding them filled with the same mud, but giving a gradual increase in depth of clear water; and as we pass on the fourth and larger lake, a scene of beauty greets us. Lovely little islands are scattered close to the shore, and the forest, one mass of living green, stretches over the mountain.

As we quietly paddle over the rippling water, a pair of loons, or great northern divers, with curiosity, slowly approach us, while the "middle," with a double-barrel, is ready to give them a warm welcome. We wait silently for either to rise on the surface to shake the water from their wings, as their custom is at times, knowing well the utter uselessness of a shot under any other circumstance. They know full well their security, for having eyed us at close quarters, one, with a gentle dip of the head, disappears under water, and then number two, with a wink and bow, bids us good-by, and we are alone on the lake. A minute passes, and then "oh-oh-o-o-o!" that strange weird laugh or cry is heard, and loon number one has come to the surface a quarter of a mile away. The cry is answered, and the half-mournful, half-exultant laugh of the second rolls the echo along the mountains, as at long rifle range he rises to shake the water from his eyes. We are sold, and the bipeds know it.

We soon find the commencement of the carry, and pitch our tent on the old camping-ground occupied by all who make the portage. Around us moose-bones are lying, and a trough hollowed from a log, evidently for the purpose of salting trout, is immediately appropriated for a wash-tub. as we think of taking in washing. Here are two large pines with part of their trunks squared, and on them are carved the names of those who have made the portage during the last fifty years. Lords from England, sportsmen from New Brunswick and the "States," trappers, hunters and Indians have passed here. We find Indian hieroglyphics, the sign of the arrow, the beaver and the moose. Here a beaver is pictured gnawing a tree, and an arrow pointing to the setting sun, and a noticing that a beaver may be found somewhere, but just where we don't know, although we should like to, for we would like a beaver to wear home.

While our molasses lasted we enjoyed the flippers that were presented at breakfast, thought well of the flappers at dinner, and did not despise the flipflaps for supper; and no matter how large a quantity was presented, each would say, "Why, I can surround that myself," but after mastering a few in great haste, a change would be perceived. The pieces would be gazed at with a more critical eye, held on the fork longer, turned about, and with great deliberation would be mastered with an effort. Then the words, "I'm partially satiated," would be heard, and the next moment the vanquished would lie back perfectly contented, sometimes even too lazy to take the fat from the frying pan or remove the plates daubed with molasses from under the elbows. Now, there is no more molasses, the jug is empty, and we use salt, pure salt, for a sauce, and we sit about the fire waiting for the first pancake to brown. Soon it is tossed to one, and the other looks with anxious and hungry eye on the favored, who swallows his share red hot and takes his turn of gazing at riches possessed by his neighbor, while the cook, with frying-pan in one hand, breaks off bits from the edges of each flipper, and fries little ones to eat on the sly.

We have caught some small trout from the lake, but these are soon gone, and as we have carried our canoe a short distance into the woods, we cannot avail ourselves of the larger trout that abound in the depths of the lake.

We stop here for rest a few, in fact a very few days, and one morning that philosopher, the Old Man, who every night had to crawl to the door of the tent, peeped as was his custom, and the next minute the cook's dreams were disturbed with "Wake up! wake up! a moose! A big black fellow, just gone over the top of a little hill! antlers eight feet broad!" Donnick is aroused with a gentle kick (nothing but a kick will arouse him, unless it be a well cooked meal, which we didn't happen to posses), and silently peeling off blankets and coats, we grasp our guns and peep from the tent to find-nothing. It was in the gray dusk of a foggy morning, and that moose had been nosing around not a dozen feet from the tent. We think it high time to be moving, if a raging moose was prowling about seeking to devour, and glad that he did not poke his head in the door and discover us, we silently push into the woods in the direction the moose has taken. We separate, each being attended by a noisy horde of red squirrels, who would run up the trees and bark, at one moment on the lower branches close to our faces, the next with a frisk of the tail in the topmost boughs, and such chattering and chippering, such anger as they showed. It was a howling wilderness, and any idiot of a moose could find us easily; but we can safely say now, that if that moose had found us, there would have death and destruction, for we were in no mood to be trifled with. As time passed, and no antlered monarch put in his appearance to pass the time of day, the Cook becoming convinced that it was safe, stepped from his hiding place behind a tree, and made for the camp.

On the way, Donnick is discovered, making for the same destination, and we enter the tent to find the Old Man safely inside, not at all frightened. Loud talk is cut short when the Cook informs them that another moose is on the other side of the little bay, and we listen to the snapping of breaking sticks and branches, as he makes his way through the wood. We tremble at this new danger (danger of striking or missing), and excitedly watch with all hands and their arms (the arms of the Cook being a revolver, an axe, and a pair of legs) and as Donnick whispers of home and "beefsteak for three," visions of fries, roasts, steaks, stews, broils, soups, broths, entrees and side dishes, flit for one brief while before us.

The moose makes a wide circuit, and the ear can plainly mark his progress, but the eye cannot discover a glimpse of him through the thick bushes, and knowing well that the slightest noise from us would send him off with the speed of the wind, we forgive him, and resignedly come back to salt, mustard and flippers.

Our coffee is prime article, so we use little of it. Rosin, soap, candles, salt pork, old boots and more, had given their essence to the water in the bottom of our canoe, and this had been filtered through our coffee bag, so that drinking at meals was about abolished by custom.

Every night after our moose adventure, one of us, sometime during the night, would be at the tent door, peeping out in hopes of discovering another, and one night the cook hearing the sploshing of water, seized a gun and looked out, expecting to find a moose walking along the edge of the lake, but it was only the waves driven the rising wind on the rocks of the shore.

Such is life. But we came for a lazy time, a life free from care; we came to breathe pure air, and we enjoy fully the little we can strain through the clouds of black flies and mosquitoes.

B.R.

Part 2:

Here is the overview of the trip as taken from George H. Reed's notes:

And a more detailed view of the camping segment:

From Bathurst

To Woodstock

Here is the transcription of the diary:

	Packet Boat Shoals about 11 AM Portland 1 hr. Eastport 1 hr. baggage [August 11] Tues AM St. J PM [August 12] Weds sus. Bridge scenery Lead mines.

🟢	**Train** This is probably how the boys got from St. John to Shediac
🟣	**Coastal Packet** Confined at P du Chene 11 hours start Fri [August 14] AM 6 o'clock R bucto at noon C & N.C. same P.M. Sat.[August 15] A.M. sunrise en route B. de Chaleur Fri A.M 14 at breakfast out of over 30 clouds beau. all Friday, British flag. Bathurst about 10. Burns, Bay View House, Rowing upriver
🔴	**1874 Canoe Route**
⛴	**Bathurst** Bot Blankets saw Lombard. Letter Roads, Living Bear on Wed. P.M. Friday took a long tramp after Partridges with H. Reed also Peters about 12 miles saw none, bad traveling through a wilderness. Eggs, black flies very numerous, also mosquitoes, saw bear & moose tracks. Sat went fishing I got 1 cod. PM to point saw nothing, slippers. People very curious stare like everything inspect closely, cheap, milk .05 Mrs. Low sent basket [August 16] Sunday heavy northwester tent stood it bravely got fossils.

Middle Landing

Left for Bathurst Sun eve with Will Knowles, jolting ride pitched tent on riverbank above the bridge. Taken for a regiment, gypsies &c people turned out to see us great ex, & very curious. H went with W to Burns store & made preparation for leaving. I, entertaining of guide at tent, who wanted a job very badly. Guides went on ahead with their canoe, we left in a team shot a partridge & pigeon on the road. Guides got there ahead at middle landing. Tried rods that eve. No success too dark. Next AM went at it early. 3 grilse and 2 salmon before breakfast. Largest 12 lbs other about 10 g's 3 &4. Rising all the time are [?] very rocky and picturesque, fine sport, canoe came after breakfast sent S to Mr. Burns. Continued fishing all forenoon till dinner. I landed my first salmon, weight 10 lbs. Total for the forenoon 4 salmon 4 grilse total weight 60 lbs. Afternoon poor luck, no rises. Total for the day same as above.

Chain of Rocks

Wed. AM no luck, H & I took canoe down stream saw S & trout. Picked hat full of blueberries PM W & H went down stream to learn how to pole a canoe, then all but me went up to Chain of Rocks in our canoe, left me to guard the tent. Returned at tea, no game.

Thurs started for C of R all hands. I walked. John 2 salmon before dinner, PM went up to little Chain, no game on a/c of storm brewing. I fish from canoe shoot little chain very many [?] When we arrived at C of R we found a nice log cabin with chains bolts &c, took possession

Grand Falls

No luck in AM. Noon left for G Falls. I walked up road. [?] blue heron 1/2 mile lost him. Went up to old camping ground saw party then went on to our place.

[August 22] Sat AM, no luck, other party left, went after partridges, no luck, lost. PM John struck 15 lb salmon broke tip of his pole Party from St. John arrived with the fish warden, no trouble about our permit.

Sun. mostly loafing all AM went down to the basin with W and took a lesson in paddling. Tried the jigs in the AM 1 Salmon out at the falls. W in canoe towed downstream some distance. Henry and I took a turn at the trout in the PM below the falls, very lively, caught 15 apiece before dark, some trouble getting back along the cliffs. A party had to stay all night there once, John thinks it has never been done before.

August 25, 1874

Tuesday A.M. broke camp and portage our things around the falls carried over narrows then left for up stream, water very low I had to jump over 16 times before supper. Made about 11 miles and camped under a large tree in a (lean-to), had an immense fire going all night, salt for snakes.

40 Mile Brook

Wed. made about 13 miles & camped at 40 mile brook. Fire ditto. Very thick woods on either side of the river, mostly spruce. John caught 2 trout for supper, one weighed 4 lbs, other 1 ½ lbs.

August 27, 1874

Thurs AM made 6 miles, river same as usual, provisions running low, only hard tack and coffee. We are 3 miles before Indian Falls and hope to portage canoe before dark. While walking along the shore I saw a number of Moosetracks, quite large, & resembles a cow.

Indian Falls

Going upriver we saw a large number of Sheldrakes, drove them ahead of us, & when we reached Indian Falls, John shot 1, which we had for supper.

At Allens Rocks, we had our first accident, W's pole slipped, H's stuck fast &d we capsized in a very swift current, & quite deep, righted the canoe & pulled it ashore, bailed it out with our hats & found we had lost only 1 bailer and W's slipper. All safe. I chased a duck just below I.F. but could not quite reach him.

Bear House

Fri. we portaged our things, & while the rest went in the canoe while I walked through the woods to the Bear House, long 3 miles, reached there about the same time as they did.

Shot 1 small partridge. At B.H. we were entertained by the men there, who gave us flippers for supper & tea bought some provisions pork, flour & molasses.

Left the guides here, and resolved to push on alone, they left in the PM & we left soon after & camped about a mile up the river, fire went out & we were quite cold in the AM.

Devil's Elbow

Sat. left for upstream, reached the Devil's Elbow at noon and camped for a day or two at least over Sunday. Splendid trout fishing, H. caught 7 good sized ones before dinner, everything dandy PM we all tried our hand at it. Henry was the most successful, total no. 16, average about 2 ½ lbs.

[August 30] Sun. raining all day PM W & I started to walk to the Bear H after more stores. Took our dep. Bearing SE by E found a path after some time, very hard & weary walk over logs & trees burnt districts, swamps, meadows & heavy undergrowth. Struck river ½ mile above & waded down sighted it at last, forded stream, completely wet through, found some flappers and had supper. Dried our clothes, had a fire all night, slept very little.

Mon. AM turned out about 4 & got our things left about 6 o'clock, things strung on a pole weighing about 50 lbs. Black flies very thick, suffered greatly from them as our hands were full & we could not drive them off. When about 1/2 way left the pole and took the things on our backs, missed the path & got into a very bad tract of country. Numerous falls, got considerable discouraged & thought some of leaving the things & pushing on alone stuck to them & about 1/2 past we sighted the knoll near camp. Pushed on completely worn out. Had to ford river. Henry had gone down to B.H. in canoe after us & arrived about 8 o'cl. Were asleep when he came. Got our things had supper & turned in completely used up. We were terribly bitten by the flies our faces were all swollen painfully.

Tues. Very stiff & lame & had late breakfast & rested all

A.M. We were very hungry this A.M. as yesterday we only had 1 flapper for breakfast, & 3 for supper the night before & our heavy tramp made us terribly hungry. Had dinner about 4 & no supper, mended clothes. H & I went out for a few moments before tea & caught 1 trout.

September 2, 1874

Wed. Broke camp & started up the river. 5 miles to dinner, soon came to B.S. Branch, went a mile beyond & camped for the night in a lean-to. Plenty of boughs & good fire. Nearest person 30 miles away, B.H. men at 42.

September 3, 1874

Thurs. Awoke covered with a heavy dew, Had managed to get outside somehow or other & got dampened accordingly. Soon after we started we came to McFarland Brook or Portage Brook, where there was an old B.H. We found a grind stone set up & ground our axe &c.

Had considerable wading to do, made 5 or 6 miles & camped in the woods about 4 as it had commenced to rain & as soon as we got the tent set up, it came down in earnest. Had fire in tent & everything went well.

September 4, 1874

Friday we made about 5 miles & camped in the remains of an old loggers camp, supposed to be about 5 miles from the lakes. Pretty hard day's work & considerable lifting to do & nearly all wading. Heard noises in eve. supposed to be those of a moose. Saw number of eagles during the day. Longfellow very useful.

Saturday. As W and I was loading the canoe just after breakfast, we saw two moose crossing the river only a little way below us. Mag. Creatures, large branching horns, dark colored & looked finely crossing the river. Got our guns & tried to head them off, but saw nothing of them, must have gone very silently.

September 5, 1874

Hard wading in river, all day long, hardly poled once, river growing smaller, camped at night in the woods.

September 6, 1874

[September 6] Sun. made early start & kept pushing on, shot a partridge. Struck first lake about 10 or 11 o'clock, very shallow & covered many feet deep with [?] Saw large number of ducks, tried to get some, by creeping, but they were too sly. Had dinner at one end, afterwards came back, found proper outlet, & pushed through to the next lake where we camped for night. W & H went back for axe, left at dinner. Saw large herons nest near camp & few ducks. Lake little deeper, but no fish.

September 7, 1874

Mon. Started across lakes, 2nd one quite round, & very pretty 3rd also, no trouble about outlets, 4th got a little astray, but soon struck right place at end of portage & camped about noon. Tried for some duck around an island, but got none, loons also. H tried for trout but got only a few small ones, about 6 miles across lakes. Names on trees, & signs of old camping place, found out the way the portage went & got rested, also washed our (W & I) clothes (birth day).

Tues. started with canoe before breakfast and carried it 1/5 of a mile. After breakfast, took some things on to where the canoe was, left them & then went on with canoe for two miles, took us till 3 or 4 to do it. Numerous rests, very hard on our shoulders, better path than we expected. ½ way found meadow & old camp. Had big supper & rested, H caught 6 or 8 trout for breakfast, not much game to be found here, so we must push on, as, we are getting short of provisions, only 4 or 5 days more of grub left, unless we shoot or fish something, which we expect to do on Tobique. Bark torches.

September 9, 1874

Wed. Early start with things. Took them through to [Br. of T.] and went back & carried canoe ¾ of a mile, then left it & went back to camp for our other things, took everything which is a pretty heavy lug. Henry shot 2 Partridge on the way, one with my revolver took time to do it. Last tote with canoe very muddy & the hardest lug of all.

Launched her & went down the brook & struck 1st lake on Tobique at dark, kept on & camped about the middle, not a very good camping ground.

September 10, 1874

Thurs. very lame & sore, late breakfast then W & I went out for partridge, no luck, black flies thirsty. Broke camp & crossed lake, made a short portage & came to Lake Victor, wind too strong to cross that night, so camped on shore. H & I tried for some trout, too dark, no luck, poor bait.

September 11, 1874

Fri. H & I went out for trout, caught 15 small ones, made a breakfast. Provisions very low, only one meal of flour left, 1 of pease & some lean pork, called it a dinner as it was rather late, mended canoe. Started to cross lake, wind strong, & lake quite long. Made outlet of Tobique & camped there. H & I tried trout got 12 small ones. Boiled ½ peas & had peas porridge & trout.

Only food left 1 meal of Pork, 1 of Flour & 1 of Pease and we are thirty miles from the nearest settlement. Intend making an early start in A.M.

September 12, 1874

Sat. boiled pork for breakfast & 2 flappers, early start. River shallow & rocky, waded all day, salt fish dinner. P.M. did some washing, helped us along, camped on river bank, think we made about 15 miles in all.

Had peas for supper & 27 trout that H caught in pools along river, only thing on hand now is 1 meal of flappers & some salt fish, growing cold, going to try to make 15 miles tomorrow which will take us to the first settlement.

3 lumbermen

[September 13] Sun. very cold last night, everything left outdoors frozen, ice 3/8 deep in pail. Eat our last meal & started, when we had made about 10 miles we came to a jam of logs, & found a shanty on shore with flour

&c set up a shout which was unexpectedly answered from the woods & soon a lumberman made his appearance & invited us up to his camp in the woods, There were 3 of them, engaged in swamping out roads & getting ready for lumbering.

They gave us a good meal, biscuits, tea, meat, gingerbread & beans. Bill took us down stream & showed us a beaver dam, got some specimens of wood. They kept a big fire going all night, & we slept very comfortably, all under one blanket some 37 ft. long. Joe, quite ingenious will be blacksmith, baker &c.

September 14, 1874

Mon. early start, they gave us something to eat, & told us that we had only made 9 miles before & were still 21 miles from McD. They thought we could make it in one day & we started.

River very crooked, saw place where beavers had been at work & got some more wood. Kept going all day & only reached the ledges at dark & camped there about 5 miles above McD's.

Did not put up the tent but slept out & very comfortable it was. Shot Partridge.

Indian Tom Noel

Tues. early start, Part. for breakfast & now nothing left to eat but expect to reach McD's before dinner. Ledges all safe, I tried walking, lost road & out of hearing of the canoe. Had to push on, had river for guide, tried to make a catamaran, but could not get the logs. Very hard walking in the woods, began to grow faint from hunger.

Hallow'd at intervals but got no response.

At last reached Forks & heard two guns, then put for them, had to ford stream, soon reached a clearing kept by Indian Tom Noel where I found the rest. Could hardly stand, limbs shook so from fatigue, increased as I neared the house, just commenced to eat some bread & molasses, when I began to faint, but managed to reach the door & lay on the grass.

Dose pain pills. Soon recovered & managed to eat a little, hard work to stop, I was so famished. Canoe suffered terribly, everything in her wet through, in my bag. After supper rest went out with Indian to spear fish. My feet were badly swollen & generally used up. We are still 3 miles from McD's. Boys returned about 10.30 result 1 salmon 15 lbs, 1 grilse about 2 & 1 doz. White fish.

Continued eating till got so I could eat without any danger, improving.

McDougall's

Wed. Patched canoe & started for McD's, reached sooner than expected, had dinner, which was prime. P.M. Aleck & O.G. helped patch our canoe, badly scraped. W. went for pitch, made us a bed in loft, slept tiptop. McD starts with us in A.M.

September 17, 1874

Thurs. O.G. undid our rods & we got off about 10.30, made good time, 3 paddles, waded only a little, made 5 or 6 miles & had dinner. P.M . met two indians Joe & John, who patched our canoe, they were going up

	Tobique hunting. They were Merashite Indians, our canoe is a Micmac. Made about 16 miles & camped at last house, had supper & slept in house before fire.
	Narrows Dam
	Chatty Woman camp Fri. early start, McD accompanying us, we had dinner near a potato patch, walked about 8 miles along road P.M. made good time with little getting out total distance 26 miles we slept on the floor of a house kept by woman, very talkative, we are 10 miles from mouth of Tobique, hope to make it by noon tomorrow. Saw ducks, Plaster Rock Mollies Table and the Highlandman's bonnet.
	September 19, 1874 Sat. Another early start, woman gave us some biscuit & potatoes. Easy paddling, canoe leaks badly, waded around Grand Bar, then came to Narrows, a narrow passage, through which the waters run with great violence McD took us through safely, though passed Indianville & came to mouth of Tobique on St. John River. I inquired at Hotel with others about fare to B. from Woodstock, 10 dollars, left McD & went about 1/2 mile down stream & camped on point, slept in mans house at night, had oatmeal for supper.
	September 20, 1874 Sun. 20. Rainy and misty, had breakfast & waited 1/2 hour for McD. Then it commenced to rain & we went up to the man`s house & staid in his barn, he gave us some

book papers &c to read & we employed the time in mending. Took us in to dinner, left after dinner, left McDs bag & dog started down stream, fine rain & fog. Paddled hard & made 15 miles from 2 till 6, camped in old red school house, W went for food & fetched [stronger ?], but noble race of men along the river hid canoe &c. Dried our clothes, people carry revolvers slept with guns

Woodstock

Mon started about 7 & paddled hard, had dinner on stream, stopped about 5 & had supper & dried our clothes, kept on paddling by moonlight quite exciting, when running the rapids, did it safely, passed time by singing. About 9 reached Woodstock distant 36 miles, tried to get past, but had to go back & camped in an unfinished house on heap of sawdust.

Train to Boston

Tues early start & paddled down to RRS had to wait some time, got baggage checked & canoe alright for 0 to USA. Train left at 930 A.M. Poor cars had dinner at McAdam, reached Bangor at dusk & had supper, took car for Boston At 12 reached Brunswick, W & I visited the college & run through them.

Wed. Slept very little til A.M. got out at Chelsea & walked to E.B. & turned out the folks. Left for Randolph on noon train

G

www.ingramcontent.com/pod-product-compliance
Lightning Source LLC
Chambersburg PA
CBHW040312010626
45792CB00022B/181